TWENTY~ONE YEARS OF THE LONDON THEATRE

With 132 photographs

Photographs by John Haynes

TAKING THE STAGE

Introduction by Lindsay Anderson

THAMES AND HUDSON

For Jane

John Haynes would like to thank Dallas Smith for all his
support and commitment, and Lindsay Anderson for his inspiration.

Half title page: Ian McKellen in *Coriolanus, see* plates 104, 116
Title page: *The Changing Room, see* plates 34, 35

First published in the USA in 1986 by Thames and Hudson Inc.,
500 Fifth Avenue, New York, New York 10110

Library of Congress Catalog Card Number 86-50515

Printed and bound in Great Britain

Introduction

I like very much a story which John Haynes told me about himself and the Royal Court Theatre. It has nothing to do with theatre photographs, but it says a lot about the Royal Court – and himself. It happened in January 1962. John was 'on the board' (operating the lighting) during a technical rehearsal for Tony Richardson's production of *A Midsummer Night's Dream*; on the stage or sitting waiting in the stalls was the typical young Royal Court company of those days – Colin Blakely (playing Bottom), Alfie Lynch (Puck), Lynn Redgrave, Rita Tushingham, David Warner, Ronnie Barker, Nicol Williamson, Samantha Eggar, Corin Redgrave . . . (how the names recall the epoch!). Jocelyn Herbert, no doubt, was wandering around with a paintbrush, touching up bits of the set. Suddenly Tony's voice rang out: 'John Osborne's being interviewed on television: we must see it. Who wants to come?' He wasn't just talking to the actors or to his friends; he was talking to everybody. 'Come back to Woodfall: we can all watch it there.' And off they all trooped to the offices of Woodfall Films in Curzon Street and watched with great amusement while John Osborne elaborated the theme of 'Damn You, England!' or some other outrageous, witty, 'angry' anti-establishment declaration. 'I knew I'd found a home,' says John Haynes.

The Royal Court, you will soon see, bulks large in this book; and not just because it is where John Haynes first started taking pictures of plays. It must bulk large in the life and work of anyone who was lucky enough to work there in its golden age – the late

5

fifties, the sixties, the early seventies. For it was a theatre unlike any other, not just in its abundance of talent, but in its unique freedom from the triviality, the competitiveness, the camp and deprecating cynicism which, alas, ran through so much London theatre. Joan Littlewood's Theatre Workshop out at Stratford East was of course another dissident group, but of quite a different character. Joan was defiantly proletarian, unliterary, 'socialist'. By contrast the Royal Court of George Devine and Tony Richardson was middle-class (not 'bourgeois'), respectful of tradition, radical rather than revolutionary, 'humanist'. And perhaps even more strongly resented. Certainly just as many seats were noisily vacated, just as many exit doors slammed during First Nights in Sloane Square as at Stratford East.

Young John Haynes was not around for those first heady days at the Court: almost certainly he was unaware of them. There was nothing theatrical – or photographic – about his background. His father had driven a bus for London Transport and retired to St Leonard's. John discovered the theatre through the weekly rep performances by the Penguin Players at the Bexhill Pavilion: a play which struck him particularly was Priestley's *Mr Kettle and Mrs Moon* – whose London première, oddly enough, had been directed by the young Tony Richardson. Its theme of an impetuous rejection of suburban life perhaps influenced John: he came to London and worked for three years in offices. He saw *The Mousetrap*.

He did his National Service as a dog-handler with the RAF Police; in Singapore he started to read plays: *The Importance of Being Earnest*, Shaw, Noël Coward, things like that. Demobbed in London, he got himself taken on – still without any conscious intention – as a stage hand at the Palace Theatre. He shifted scenery for musicals: he trained a follow-spot on Benny Hill. But something told him that this was not the kind of theatre in which he could happily spend his life.

What he had read or heard about the Royal Court stirred his interest. He wrote and asked for a job. He got one. It meant demotion from 'first dayman' to 'second dayman' and it meant a drop in salary. But he took it.

And about this time something else happened, just as crucial. He was given a book of photographs by Cartier-Bresson, *The Europeans*, and his eyes were opened. He decided to be a photographer. His father gave him a Leica and he started roaming the streets, trying to capture significant fragments of living. To make some extra money, he took portraits of actors: but that he did not enjoy. Then Keith Johnstone, who ran a mime class at the Court, suggested he take a few pictures of that. George Devine came along sometimes to talk about a subject dear to his heart: the use of the mask. And so the first picture in this book was taken – a touching and characteristic portrait of the man to whom we owe, more than to anyone else, the achievement of the Royal Court. The man to whom (as he put it) the theatre was a temple, not a whorehouse. It is the kind of portrait John Haynes takes best: a personality revealed in action, the artist exposed.

The conjunction of his two prime influences did not, however, lead John directly to taking pictures of plays. He got married – he met his wife Jane, an actress, when attending Keith Johnstone's class – and he had to earn a living. He decided to try journalism. For two years he worked as a photographer for *The Sunday Times*, where you were (in his words) 'out there in the front line, living on your nerves'. But the pursuit of politicians, strikers and headline personalities proved not much more congenial than the follow-spot at the Palace: John is neither a thruster nor a manipulator. There are times, though, when the theatre calls for persistence, insistence and a tough hide, so probably the experience was good for him. Anyway, when the Royal Court decided in 1970 to appoint a regular theatre photographer, he had enough confidence to apply for the job. He got it. His first assignment was David Storey's *Home*, which I was directing with that unequalled cast, a play with almost no action and a great deal of poetry. John's pictures were simple, responsive, unerring – the theatrical experience exactly. He had found his *métier*.

Photographers have a hard time in the theatre. Their opportunities, you may think, are rich. What effects of lighting and décor offer themselves! What expressive plasticity! What personalities, what emotions, what moments of gaiety, pathos, violence! . . . Alas, all too often these apparently limitless possibilities create only frustration for the photographers of theatre. They are there, and they must never forget it, for a practical purpose, generally one sufficiently defined by the word 'publicity'. Pictures are wanted for the press – and will the artistes please stand a bit closer together, otherwise those on the edges are likely to find themselves cropped out of the group. Pictures are wanted for display outside the theatre, to entice passing trade. Pictures are wanted to satisfy the players, who naturally want to look good. Whether directors or managements value the photographer's contribution depends on how much they care about permanence in this most transient of the arts. Generally they don't care very much. (And they don't pay much either.)

Time is the photographer's worst enemy. Usually he has to work in those tense, crowded hours between dress rehearsal and first performance, when tempers are short and nerves are strained. Nowadays he will be lucky if he is given a session to himself on stage and with the actors, and if he is it will be too short – particularly if the production involves changes of scene and costume. No wonder the custom has grown more prevalent for the pictures to be taken during dress rehearsals, from the auditorium. This at least ensures authenticity, spontaneity. But there are dangers, too. More than one star has suddenly broken off in the middle of a scene, peered angrily into the darkness where the photographer is busily clicking away, and shouted: 'Get that damned cameraman out of here!'

Most theatre photographers now – and John Haynes is no exception – work with 35 mm cameras, hand-held most of the time, and with available light, i.e. the lighting designed for the production. They will very likely persuade the Chief Electrician to bump up his levels a bit, but gone are the days when every shot was carefully composed and specially lit. This is another aspect of the freedom won by the 1956 revolution, pioneered like so much else by the Royal Court. I remember vividly Julie Hamilton's pictures, daring now, of Angus Wilson's *The Mulberry Bush*, which opened the Court's first season. Full of life, informal and unposed, they were the first professional theatre pictures taken on 35 mm I had ever seen: quite possibly they were the first altogether. They reflected brilliantly and refreshingly the new styles of writing and playing – direct, contemporary, unglossed – which were invading the stage. Gone was the shop-window elegance of grouping and posture which had come to reflect an in-the-main snobby and artificial West End style. This was a theatre in which a young photographer with Cartier-Bresson leanings could feel he had a place.

Admittedly there has been a small loss with the huge gain. We don't often get full-stage shots of contemporary productions, with the characters in their settings, as you would see them from a centre stall or the front of the circle. (There are only four, I think, in this book.) Today's photographers are not interested in such pictures chiefly, I suppose, because newspapers would not print them. And it is worth remembering the special effect on theatre pictures of the general use of available light. Fast film can capture the actors satisfactorily enough; but there is rarely enough light on décor to record the stage

Home
David Storey
Royal Court Theatre, 1970
Directed by Lindsay Anderson

Left
Standing: John Gielgud,
Ralph Richardson
Seated: Mona Washbourne,
Warren Clarke, Dandy Nichols

Far left
Standing: Alan Price (music),
Andy Philips (lighting)
Seated: David Storey,
Lindsay Anderson,
Jocelyn Herbert (design)

picture as the audience sees it. Low-key images are the result, with the actors highlit in a more dramatic way than they are in performance. What we see is a concentration, an intensification of the theatrical moment.

The photographer's role in the theatre has in fact become more personal, more creative, less that of a recorder or glamorizer. For *The Sunday Times* John Haynes worked as a journalist: he went out to find the pictures he had been ordered to get. When he returned to the Court he found himself expected to function as an artist, which fortunately he had been without exactly knowing it. From the start he was encouraged to take time, and he was lucky enough to be photographing the work of an author to whom he responded so deeply. The 'still, sad' (sometimes raucous) 'music of humanity' which is what makes *Home* such a great play, as well as the special genius of its performers, struck a chord in John which resounds in his photographs: and I would say the same of his pictures of *The Changing Room*, *Life Class* and *Early Days*. Indeed, his imagination was so stirred by this contact with David Storey's peculiarly Northern world of poetry that he set off to the North of England himself and made a lovely set of pictures which we showed in an exhibition at the Court. Nothing – and everything – to do with the theatre. Perhaps one day he will make a book of them.

John Haynes' photographs show, as any collection of stage pictures must, an extraordinary and attractive variety. But in the best of them there is always this acute, tender human response: he is not a pictorialist or a publicist, he is an artist. Of course this book is an anthology. John has enough pictures to fill these pages many times over; and there are many theatres in London where he did not work, many productions over those years which he was not invited to

Barry Copley, David Daker
and Mark McManus
The Changing Room
David Storey
Royal Court Theatre
1971
Directed by
Lindsay Anderson

photograph. But not many of our finest players have escaped him. Here they nearly all are, holding the mirror up to our time and our nature with the accuracy and courage with which actors and actresses are so generously gifted. God bless them!

I have often wondered at the different images people have of the theatre, and the difference of their experience of it. It can speak with so many voices, such different accents. It can be trivial and it can be wise; it can soothe and it can disturb; it can flatter and it can teach. To one distinguished director, who was not speaking in anger, it is a 'whorehouse'. To George Devine it was a 'temple' – remembering that a temple is a place for joy as well as reverence. In all its variety, the London theatre seems to me to embody most distinctly these two traditions: the tradition of *show* and the tradition of *truth*. Some productions illustrate: critics call this 'conceptual theatre' and they like it because they find it easy to write about, bright pupils sitting down before exam papers. But some productions offer the challenge of feeling, of involvement. This is the theatre of experience, and it is not easy to write about. It is this theatre to which John Haynes has belonged, and belongs: he pictures the temple, not the whorehouse. It is a theatre I recognize and honour. These pictures make me glad to have been a part of it.

LINDSAY ANDERSON
April 1986

1
George Devine, 1964

'For me, the theatre is really
a religion or way of life.
You must decide what you
feel the world is about
and what you want to say
about it, so that everything
in the theatre you work in
is saying the same thing. . . .
If you can't find one you
like, start one of your own.'

2 Bernard Gallagher as
Andreyevesky
Bolsover Griffiths
The Cresta Run
N. F. Simpson
Royal Court Theatre, 1965
Directed by Keith Johnstone

3 Jill Bennett as Anna Bowers
Diana Dors as Mrs Hanker
Three Months Gone
Donald Howarth
Royal Court Theatre, 1970
Directed by Ronald Eyre

4 Tom Bell as Horst
Ian McKellen as Max
Bent
Martin Sherman
Royal Court Theatre, 1979
Directed by Robert Chetwyn

5
Mike Pratt as Luther
Gascoigne
The Daughter-in-Law
D. H. Lawrence
Royal Court Theatre
1967
Directed by Peter Gill

6
Hugh Fraser as Peyote
Helen Mirren as Maggie
Teeth 'n Smiles
David Hare
Royal Court Theatre, 1975
Directed by the author

7
Josh Cruze as Doc
Richard Chaves as Dicky Dau
Vincent Caristi as Baby Fan
Brian Delate as Little John
Tracers
Devised and directed by
John DiFusco
Vietnam Veterans Ensemble
Theatre Upstairs, Royal Court, 1985

8
Leon Vitali as Ansome
Michael Kitchen as Mask
Michael Grady as Kitchen
Nigel Terry as Knife
Big Wolf
Harald Mueller
Royal Court Theatre, 1972
Directed by William Gaskill with
Pam Brighton

9
John Gielgud as Harry
Ralph Richardson as Jack
Home
David Storey
Royal Court Theatre, 1970
Directed by Lindsay Anderson

10
John Kani as Styles
Winston Ntshona as
Sizwe Bansi
Sizwe Bansi is Dead
Athol Fugard
Theatre Upstairs, Royal
Court, 1973
Directed by the author

11 Yvonne Bryceland as Lena
Boesman and Lena
Athol Fugard
Theatre Upstairs, Royal Court, 1971
Directed by the author

12 Tony London as Nipper
Michael Deeks as Sweetheart
Phil Daniels as Iron
Peter-Hugo Daly as Sky-light
Class Enemy
Nigel Williams
Theatre Upstairs, Royal Court, 1978
Directed by William Alexander

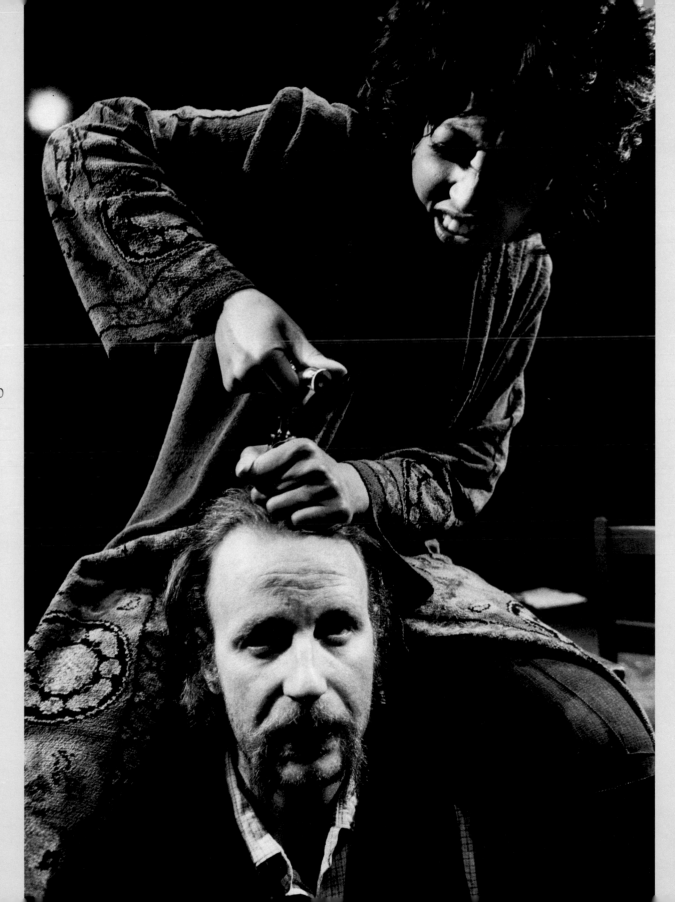

13
Sheila Scott-Wilkinson
as Sadie
Victor Henry as Perowne
AC/DC
Heathcote Williams
Royal Court Theatre 1970
Directed by Nicholas
Wright

14 Julian Wadham
The Falkland Sound
Conceived and directed by Max Stafford-Clark
Theatre Upstairs, Royal Court, 1983

15
Jennie Stoller as Val
Tricia Kelly as Becky
Amelda Brown as Angela
Fen
Caryl Churchill
Joint Stock Theatre Group
Royal Court Theatre, 1983
Directed by Les Waters

16
Billie Whitelaw as Winnie
Happy Days
Samuel Beckett
Royal Court Theatre, 1979
Directed by the author

17
Peggy Ashcroft as Claire Lannes
The Lovers of Viorne
Marguerite Duras
Royal Court Theatre, 1971
Directed by Jonathan Hales

18 Joint Stock Theatre Group
Victory
Howard Barker
Royal Court Theatre, 1983
Directed by Danny Boyle

19
Tom Wilkinson as
T. S. Eliot
Julie Covington as
Vivien Eliot
Tom and Viv
Michael Hastings
Royal Court Theatre
1984
Directed by
Max Stafford-Clark

20
Stuart Brisley's
**A Celebration for
Due Process**
at **Come Together**
A Festival of New Work
Royal Court Theatre, 1970

21 John Osborne, 1976

22
Max Wall as Archie Rice
The Entertainer
John Osborne
Greenwich Theatre, 1974
Directed by the author

23
Michael Gough as
Baron Von Epp
Alan Bates as Alfred Redl
A Patriot for Me
John Osborne
Theatre Royal, Haymarket
1983
Directed by Ronald Eyre

24
Ralph Michael as
Grandfather
Rachel Kempson as
Older Lady
A Sense of Detachment
John Osborne
Royal Court Theatre, 1972
Directed by Frank Dunlop

25
Stephen Rea as Clov
Patrick Magee as Hamm
Endgame
Samuel Beckett
Royal Court Theatre
1976
Directed by
Donald McWhinnie

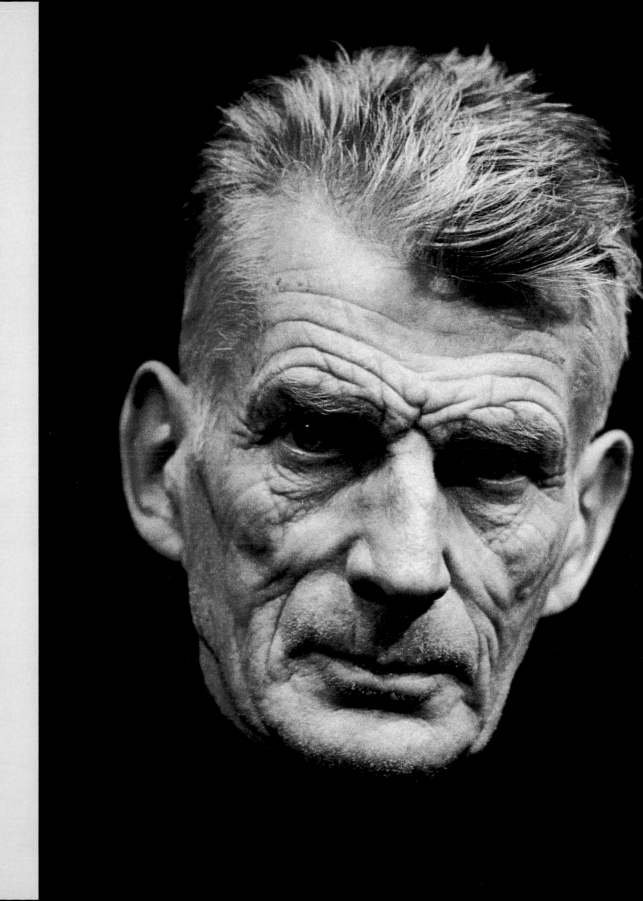

27 Billie Whitelaw as the Mouth
Not I
Samuel Beckett
Royal Court Theatre, 1973
Directed by Anthony Page

28
Billie Whitelaw as May
Footfalls
Samuel Beckett
Royal Court Theatre, 1976
Directed by the author

30 David Storey, 1972

29 Stuart Rayner as Mooney
Brenda Cavendish as Gillian
Alan Bates as Allott
Frank Grimes as Saunders
David Lincoln as Carter
Paul Kelly as Mathews
Life Class
David Storey
Royal Court Theatre, 1974
Directed by Lindsay Anderson

Home
David Storey
Royal Court Theatre, 1970
Directed by
Lindsay Anderson

31
Dandy Nichols as Marjorie
Ralph Richardson as Jack

32
John Gielgud as Harry
Mona Washbourne as Kathleen

33
Ralph Richardson as Jack
John Gielgud as Harry

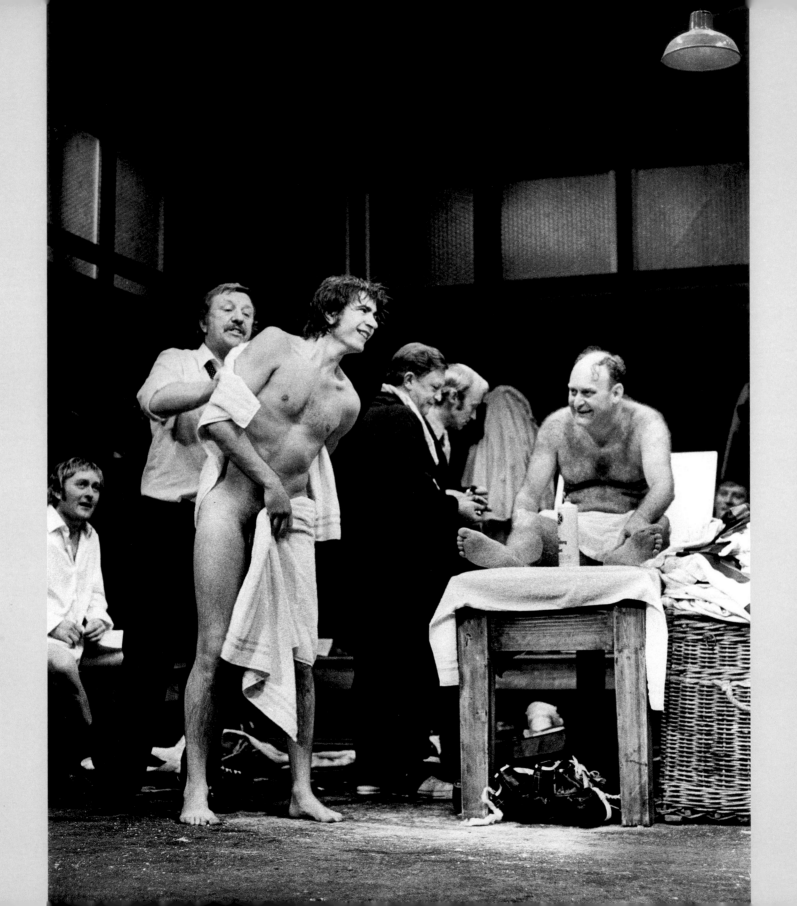

The Changing Room
David Storey
Royal Court Theatre, 1971
Directed by Lindsay Anderson

34
Peter Childs as Fenchurch
Barry Keegan as Danny Crosby
John Price as Frank Moore
Don McKillop as Luke
Jim Norton as Patsy
Peter Schofield as Bryan Atkinson

35 The City
Standing: Don McKillop, Brian Glover, John Price, David Hill,
David Daker, Barry Keegan, Peter Schofield, Warren Clarke, Peter
Childs, Alun Armstrong, John Rae, John Barrett, Brian Lawson
Seated: Matthew Guinness, Jim Norton, Edward Judd, Frank Mills, Paul
Dawkins, Michael Elphick, Mark McManus, Edward Peel,
Geoffrey Hinsliff

36 Edward Bond, 1985

37 Gerard Horan as Pete
Saved
Edward Bond
Royal Court Theatre, 1985
Directed by Danny Boyle

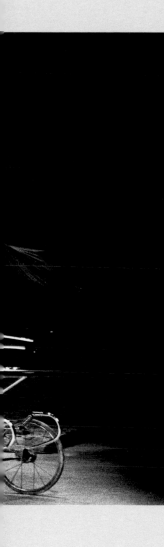

38
Harry Andrews in
the title role
Lear
Edward Bond
Royal Court Theatre
1971
Directed by
William Gaskill

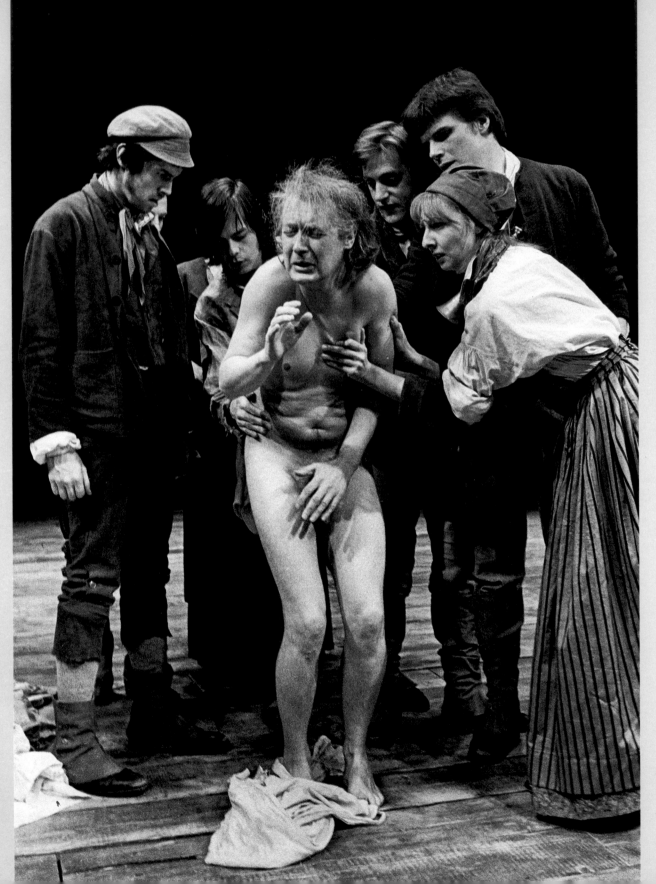

39
Nigel Terry as Darkie
Roderick Smith as Bob
John Normington
as Parson
David Troughton as Miles
Malcolm Ingram as Peter
Sheila Kelly as Betty
The Fool
Edward Bond
Royal Court Theatre, 1975
Directed by Peter Gill

40 Gillian Martell as Jessica Tilehouse
Margaret Lawley as Davis
Adrienne Byrne as Jilly
Coral Browne as Louise Rafi
Alan Webb as Evens
Susan Williamson as Mafanwy Price
Barbara Ogilvie as Rachel
The Sea
Edward Bond
Royal Court Theatre, 1973
Directed by William Gaskill

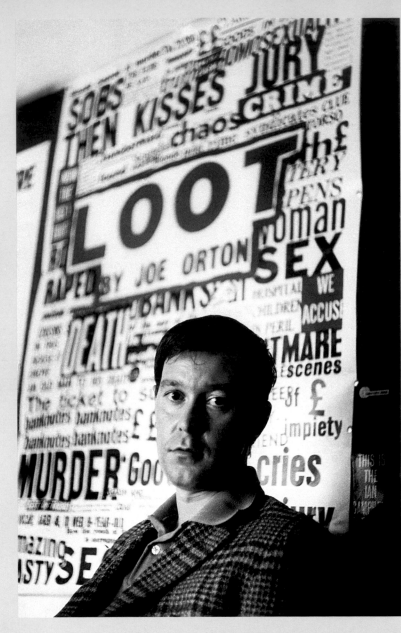

41 Joe Orton, 1966

42 Beryl Reid as Kath
Malcolm McDowell as Mr Sloane
Entertaining Mr Sloane
Joe Orton
Royal Court Theatre, 1975
Directed by Roger Croucher

43 Liv Ullmann as Anna
Old Times
Harold Pinter
Theatre Royal, Haymarket, 1985
Directed by David Jones

44
Harold Pinter, 1971

45
Roger Lloyd Pack as Joey
The Homecoming
Harold Pinter
Garrick Theatre, 1978
Directed by Kevin Billington

46 Warren Mitchell as Davies
The Caretaker
Harold Pinter
National Theatre, 1980
Directed by Kenneth Ives

47
Michael Kitchen as Lenny
Timothy West as Max
The Homecoming
Harold Pinter
Garrick Theatre, 1978
Directed by Kevin Billington

48
Warren Clarke as Blue Morphan
Richard O'Brien as Willie
The Unseen Hand
Sam Shepard
Theatre Upstairs, Royal Court
1973
Directed by Jim Sharman

50
Julie Walters as May
Ian Charleson as Eddie
Fool for Love
Sam Shepard
National Theatre, 1984
Directed by Peter Gill

49
Bob Hoskins as Beaujo
Stephen Rea as Cody
Geography of a Horse Dreamer
Sam Shepard
Theatre Upstairs, Royal Court
1974
Directed by the author

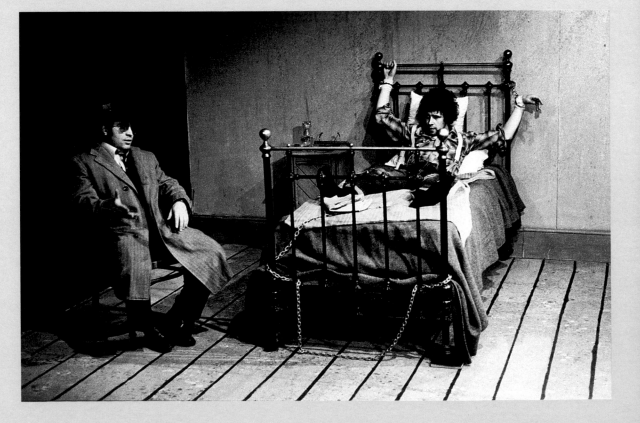

51 Jonathan Pryce in the title role
Hamlet
William Shakespeare
Royal Court Theatre, 1980
Directed by Richard Eyre

52
Anton Lesser and
Judy Buxton in the title roles
Romeo and Juliet
William Shakespeare
Royal Shakespeare Company
Barbican Theatre, 1981
Directed by Ron Daniels

53 Harriet Walter as Helena
Peggy Ashcroft as Countess of Rousillon
All's Well That Ends Well
William Shakespeare
Royal Shakespeare Company
Barbican Theatre, 1982
Directed by Trevor Nunn

54 Alec Guinness in the title role
Simone Signoret as Lady Macbeth
Macbeth
William Shakespeare
Royal Court Theatre, 1966
Directed by William Gaskill

55 Bob Todd as the Gravedigger
Frank Grimes in the title role
Hamlet
William Shakespeare
Theatre Royal, Stratford East, 1981
Directed by Lindsay Anderson

56
Victor Henry as Daniel de Bosola
Judy Parfitt in the title role
The Duchess of Malfi
John Webster
Royal Court Theatre, 1971
Directed by Peter Gill

57
Ian McKellen in the title role
Susan Dury, Judith Harte and
Marie Kean
as the Three Witches
Macbeth
William Shakespeare
Royal Shakespeare Company
Young Vic Theatre, 1978
Directed by Trevor Nunn

58
Glenda Jackson as Vittoria
Corombona
Jack Shepherd as Flamineo
The White Devil
John Webster
Old Vic Theatre, 1976
Directed by
Michael Lindsay-Hogg

59 Vanessa Redgrave as Arkadina
Jonathan Pryce as Trigorin
The Seagull
Anton Chekhov
Queen's Theatre, 1985
Directed by Charles Sturridge

60 Ian McKellen as Platinov
Wild Honey
Anton Chekhov, adapted by Michael Frayn
National Theatre, 1984
Directed by Christopher Morahan

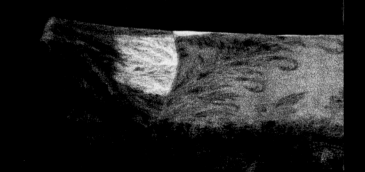

61
Marianne Faithfull as Irina
The Three Sisters
Anton Chekhov
Royal Court Theatre, 1967
Directed by
William Gaskill

62
Jill Bennett
as Hedda Tesman
Hedda Gabler
Henrik Ibsen
Royal Court Theatre, 1972
Directed by Anthony Page

63
Rik Mayall as Ivan
Khlestakov
Jim Broadbent as Anton
Svoznik-Dmuchanovsky
**The Government
Inspector**
Nikolai Gogol
National Theatre
1985
Directed by Richard
Eyre

64 Beryl Reid as Donna Katherina
Peggy Mount as Donna Pasqua
Il Campiello
Carlo Goldoni
National Theatre, 1976
Directed by Bill Bryden

65
Penelope Wilton as Barbara Undershaft
Major Barbara
George Bernard Shaw
National Theatre, 1982
Directed by Peter Gill

66 Frances de la Tour as Joan
Saint Joan
George Bernard Shaw
National Theatre, 1984
Directed by Ronald Eyre

67 Bill Paterson as Schweik
Jim Carter as Hitler
Schweik in the Second World War
Bertolt Brecht
National Theatre, 1982
Directed by Richard Eyre

68
Frank Grimes as
Christy Mahon

Playboy of the Western World
J. M. Synge
Riverside Studios, 1984
Directed by Lindsay Anderson

69 Eve Matheson as Susan Brady
Marian McLoughlin as Sarah Tansey
Lisa Cook as Honour Blake

70
Lauren Bacall as the
Princess
Kosmonopolis
Sweet Bird of Youth
Tennessee Williams
Theatre Royal, Haymarket
1985
Directed by Harold Pinter

A Streetcar Named Desire
Tennessee Williams
Piccadilly Theatre, 1974
Directed by Edwin Sherin

71 Martin Shaw as Stanley Kowalski

72 Claire Bloom as Blanche Dubois

73
Laurence Olivier as John Tagg
The Party
Trevor Griffiths
National Theatre, 1973
Directed by John Dexter

Home
David Storey
Royal Court Theatre, 1970
Directed by Lindsay Anderson

74
John Gielgud as Harry

75
Ralph Richardson as Jack

76
Maggie Smith as Connie
Snap
Charles Lawrence
Vaudeville Theatre, 1974
Directed by William Gaskill

77
Alec Guinness as Hilary
The Old Country
Alan Bennett
Queen's Theatre, 1977
Directed by Clifford
Williams

78
Lucinda Macdonald as
a Mannequin
Paul Scofield as
Constantine Madras
The Madras House
Harley Granville-Barker
National Theatre, 1977
Directed by
William Gaskill

79
Paul Scofield as Alan
West
Savages
Christopher Hampton
Royal Court Theatre
1973
Directed by
Robert Kidd

Alpha Beta
E. A. Whitehead
Royal Court Theatre, 1972
Directed by Anthony Page

80
Rachel Roberts as Mrs Elliot

81 Albert Finney as Mr Elliot

82
Joan Plowright as
Connie Craven
Enjoy
Alan Bennett
Vaudeville Theatre, 1980
Directed by Ronald Eyre

83 Alan Bates as Ben Butley
Butley
Simon Gray
Criterion Theatre, 1971
Directed by Harold Pinter

84
Roy Dotrice as John Aubrey
Brief Lives
John Aubrey
Hampstead Theatre Club
1967
Directed by Patrick
Garland

85
Wendy Morgan in
the title role
Martine
Jean-Jacques Bernard
National Theatre, 1985
Directed by Peter Hall

86
Mona Washbourne
as Aunt
Glenda Jackson
as Stevie Smith
Stevie
Hugh Whitemore
Vaudeville Theatre, 1977
Directed by
Clifford Williams

87 Alastair Sim as Willy
Siege
David Ambrose
Cambridge Theatre, 1972
Directed by Robert Kidd

88
Peter Firth as Alan Strang
Equus
Peter Shaffer
National Theatre, 1973
Directed by John Dexter

89 Daniel Day Lewis as Guy Bennett
Another Country
Julian Mitchell
Queen's Theatre, 1983
Directed by Stuart Burge

90 Tim Curry as Frank 'n furter
The Rocky Horror Show
Richard O'Brien
Theatre Upstairs, Royal Court, 1973
Directed by Jim Sharman

91
Antony Sher as
Arnold Beckoff
Torch Song Trilogy
Harvey Fierstein
Albery Theatre, 1985
Directed by Robert Allan
Ackerman

92 Rachel Kempson as Blanche
Margaret Leighton as Matty Seaton
Graham Swannell as Mark
Bruce Bold as Clement
Anthony Nicholls as Edgar Gaveston
Alec Guinness as Dudley
Nicola Pagett as Justine
Donald Eccles as Oliver Seaton
A Family and a Fortune
Julian Mitchell, based on
Ivy Compton-Burnett
Apollo Theatre, 1975
Directed by Alan Strachan

93
Anthony May and the
National Youth Theatre
Zigger Zagger
Peter Terson
Jeannetta Cochrane Theatre
1967
Directed by Michael Croft

94
Felicity Kendal as Dottie
Jumpers
Tom Stoppard
Aldwych Theatre, 1985
Directed by Peter Wood

95 Anthony Allen as Richard
Philomena McDonagh as Thomasina
Crystal Clear
Devised and directed by Phil Young
Wyndham Theatre, 1983

96 John Standing as Benedict
Annie Leon as Daisy
Michael Redgrave as Jasper
Close of Play
Simon Gray
National Theatre, 1979
Directed by Harold Pinter

97
Alan Bennett as Mrs Swabb
Mike Carnell as Mr Shanks
Habeas Corpus
Alan Bennett
Lyric Theatre, 1973
Directed by Ronald Eyre

98
Robin Bailey as Eddie
Loomis
Edward Fox as St John
Quartermaine
Quartermaine's Terms
Simon Gray
Lyric Theatre, 1981
Directed by
Harold Pinter

101
June Page as Mary McGinty
Anna Keaveney as Mary Gallagher
Jane Carr as Mary Mooney
Once a Catholic
Mary O'Malley
Royal Court Theatre, 1977
Directed by Mike Ockrent

102 Cheryl Kennedy as Joan
Tom Courtenay as Leonard
Time and Time Again
Alan Ayckbourn
Comedy Theatre, 1972
Directed by Eric Thompson

103
John Gielgud as Sir Geoffrey Kendle
Bob Hoskins as Bernie the Volt
Veterans
Charles Wood
Royal Court Theatre, 1972
Directed by Ronald Eyre

104
Coriolanus
William Shakespeare
National Theatre, 1984
Directed by Peter Hall

105
Kate Locke as Amy
Kissing God
Devised and directed by Phil Young
Hampstead Theatre, 1984

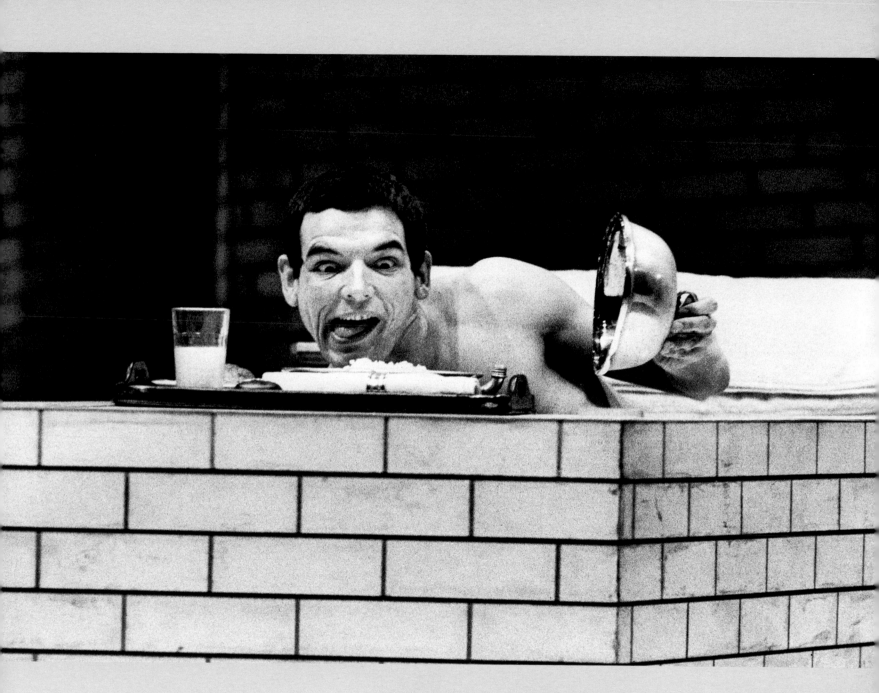

106 David Scofield as John Merrick
The Elephant Man
Bernard Pomerance
National Theatre, 1980
Directed by Roland Rees

107
Stephen Greif as Biff
Warren Mitchell as Willie Loman
David Baxt as Happy
Death of a Salesman
Arthur Miller
National Theatre, 1979
Directed by Michael Rudman

108
Russell Boulter as Richard
**The Life and Death of
Richard III**
Devised and directed by
Christopher G. Sandford
From William Shakespeare
LAMDA, Macowan Theatre
1984

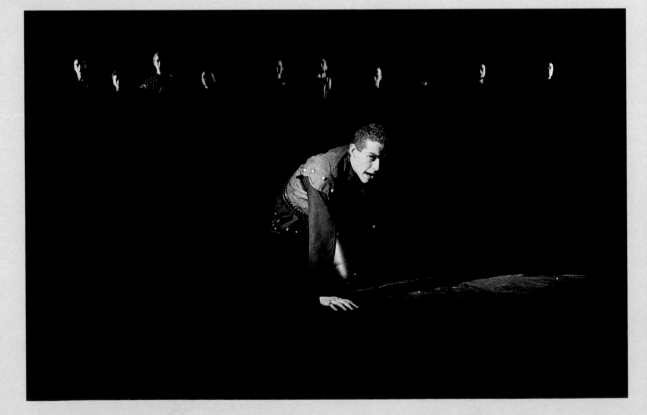

109
Selina Cadell as
Mrs Drudge
Roy Kinnear as Birdboot
Edward Petherbridge
as Moon
**The Real Inspector
Hound**
Tom Stoppard
National Theatre, 1985
Directed by the author

110
Diana Rigg as Ruth Carson
Night and Day
Tom Stoppard
Phoenix Theatre, 1978
Directed by Peter Wood

111 Janet McTeer as Mary
The Grace of Mary Traverse
Timberlake Wertenbaker
Royal Court Theatre, 1985
Directed by Danny Boyle

112 Alan Bates in the title role
Yonadab
Peter Shaffer
National Theatre, 1985
Directed by Peter Hall

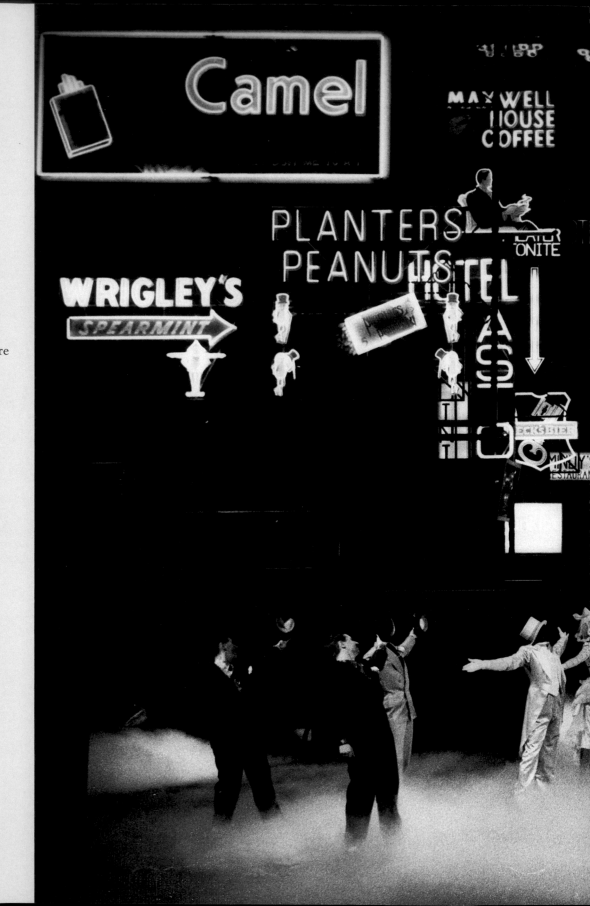

114 William Gaskill directs
Big Wolf
Harald Mueller
Royal Court Theatre, 1972

115 Joint Stock Theatre Group rehearsing
David Hare's
Fanshen, 1975
Directed by William Gaskill and Max Stafford-Clark

116
Peter Hall directs Ian McKellen
Coriolanus
William Shakespeare
National Theatre, 1984

117
John Dexter and Arnold Wesker
at rehearsal of Wesker's
The Old Ones
Royal Court Theatre, 1972

118
Peter Gill directs his own play
Small Change
Riverside Studios, 1977

119
Billie Whitelaw and Samuel Beckett
at rehearsal of Beckett's
Footfalls
Royal Court Theatre, 1976

120
David Storey and Ralph Richardson
at rehearsal of Storey's
Early Days
National Theatre, 1980

121
John Gielgud as Sir Geoffrey Kendle
Veterans (rehearsal)
Charles Wood
Royal Court Theatre, 1972
Directed by Ronald Eyre

122 Nicol Williamson as Malvolio
Twelfth Night (rehearsal)
William Shakespeare
Royal Shakespeare Company
Aldwych Theatre, 1975
Directed by Peter Gill

124 Richard Eyre, 1984

123
Michael Rudman and
Carl Toms
discuss designs
For Services Rendered
Somerset Maugham
National Theatre, 1979

125
Ralph Richardson, Dandy Nichols,
Warren Clarke, John Gielgud
and Mona Washbourne rehearsing
Home
David Storey
Royal Court Theatre, 1970
Directed by Lindsay Anderson

126 Lindsay Anderson, 1973

127 Ralph Richardson and
Jill Bennett rehearsing
West of Suez
John Osborne
Royal Court Theatre, 1971
Directed by Anthony Page

Index

Numbers in *italic* refer to page numbers; numbers in roman refer to photographs.